1·50

Remember Me:

A Meditation on the Stations of the Cross

Brother Ramon SSF

GW00384713

Marshall Pickering

Marshall Morgan and Scott
Marshall Pickering
3 Beggarwood Lane, Basingstoke, Hants RG23 7LP, UK

Illustrations copyright © 1979 by the Benedictine Nuns of Cockfosters
Copyright © 1988 Brother Ramon SSF
First published in 1988 by Marshall Morgan and Scott Publications Ltd
Part of the Marshall Pickering Holdings Group
A subsidiary of the Zondervan Corporation

British Library CIP Data

Ramon, *Brother*
   Remember me: the Stations of the Cross.
   —(Evangelical spirituality series).
   1. Stations of the Cross—Meditations
   I. Title   II. Series
   232.9′6 BX2040

   ISBN 0-551-01542-X

Text set in Baskerville by Brian Robinson, Buckingham
Printed in Great Britain by Henry Ling Ltd., at the Dorset Press,
Dorchester, Dorset

Contents

☐ CHRISTIAN SPIRITUALITY SERIES ☐

What are the Stations of the Cross?

This Prologue is written with newcomers in mind. I mean those who have never seen, known or experienced the Stations of the Cross. If you are one of these, then let me explain a little of what it is all about, and commend such a devotion to you for use privately (using this book), corporately with a group of friends who are experimenting with new forms of prayer and devotion, or in a church where the Stations of the Cross are permanently displayed for personal and corporate use.

First of all let me say that this devotion is one way in which the desire of the apostle Paul may be concretely expressed: '. . . that I may know him, and the power of his resurrection, and may share his sufferings, becoming like him in his death . . .' (Phil. 3:10). It is an actual participation in the pilgrimage which Jesus made on the road to Calvary. It is an entering with him, and enacting by faith those stations on the way, and seeking to be identified with that last journey which led him to the cross for our sakes. Walking the stations, you use your body and mind in prayer, and your spirit is joined to the suffering Jesus on his way to Calvary.

This book has been put together so that you alone or with your friends, or in the company of a larger congregation, can actually 'walk the Stations'. It is a bodily, as well as a mental and spiritual sharing on the road to Calvary. The simplest thing to do, first of all, is to go into an Anglican or a Roman Catholic Church which displays the Stations, and look at them. Identify the pictures with the numbers in this book, and get to know them. You may find that there are only fourteen Stations traditionally depicted. It is now the custom to add the fifteenth

Station, because although we live in the shadow of Calvary on Good Friday, nevertheless, we do live 'this side of Easter', and Jesus is no longer on the cross!

Each Station depicts in stone, wood or paint, one of the incidents on the Calvary road. At each Station you stop, reflect, meditate, pray, pause,—and then sing or recite the verse which brings you to the next Station, and this is repeated for the fifteen Stations.

You may choose to walk and pray the Stations in a Church,—don't be nervous about it, because that is why they are there! Obviously, if you are alone you will pray quietly, and if you are sharing the devotion with friends, you should ask permission, because the devotion will then be audible, and others may want to use the church for silent prayer. If you join an ongoing liturgical observation of the practice during Lent, then there is no problem.

If you do not use a church or other building, then you will need to mark the Stations. The simplest way is to mark the numbers 1–15 with a large felt pen and place or paste them some distance from each other in a garden, field or private place. When I walked the Stations on a mountain, I selected fifteen large stones, placed well apart, and pasted the numbers on the stones. The fifteenth Station was a mound of small stones surmounted by a rough, empty cross, where I knelt for a long period of silence at the end of the devotion. Obviously, this needs preparation beforehand.

When should you do it? Well Fridays are appropriate, and the season of Lent is appropriate, and Good Friday is especially appropriate. But the value of a book like this is that it can be taken up at any time, and the devotion can be done in your own room without moving. But I would encourage you to actually walk,—make the pilgrimage and try to get some experience of doing it with others.

I say I have written this Prologue for newcomers. It is not written to compromise your own tradition or to lead you into another, but simply to introduce you to a devotion and practice which can enrich your life of prayer and devotion. The next page begins with me sitting in the enclosed garden of our Glasshampton monastery last Good Friday morning, just after the brothers and guests had walked the Stations of the Cross, and that is a good vantage point from which to invite you to make the pilgrimage with Jesus through his sorrows, and into the glory of his risen life.

To be a Pilgrim

I write these words on Good Friday morning in the garth of the monastery of St Mary at the Cross. Last evening we celebrated the Last Supper, and after the reading of the Gospel in St John 13:1–17 brothers and guests had their feet washed according to our Saviour's words. Then a Gethsemane watch was set up until midnight, anticipating the profound sadness of this day, which is nevertheless shot through with the hope of glory.

This is the day on which we remember the suffering and pain of Jesus, and yet the sun is shining and an abundance of flowers and budding trees surround me. We have just finished the pilgrimage of the Stations of the Cross, and all around the monastery and here in the garth the large illustrations of the stations by the Benedictine nuns of Cockfosters add to the still sadness of the day. I am surrounded, also, by birdsong which is quite compatible with Good Friday meditation, for however deeply I enter into the way of sorrows, it is at the cross that light and joy and hope shine forth in gospel radiance.

Early this morning one of the friars set up the fifteen stations of the cross, which depict the *Via Dolorosa*, the Way of the Cross, from Jesus' condemnation to death before Pilate to the anticipation of his glorious rising from the dead. Then after Morning Prayer, friars and guests followed the way to Calvary, not only in company with pilgrims in Jerusalem this Good Friday, but with Christians throughout the world who seek a gospel conformity to our Lord Jesus Christ in his sufferings and glory.

At noon we shall gather in the Chapel to share the last three hours of our Lord's earthly life, and a strange stillness will pervade the monastery until we meet before dawn on Easter Sunday morning to celebrate with light and fire, with bread and wine, with word and sacrament, the glorious risen presence of Jesus in our midst—immortal life released for the healing and salvation of the world.

But I am anticipating, for as I write in the garden this morning, I am held by the Holy Spirit in the sadness of Calvary, in an awareness of the cost of our redemption in shed blood, sweat and mortal agony.

Because this morning has been so precious, I want to share it. The two friars who read the meditations on the passion at each station were aware of the meaning and implication of their readings. Professed brothers, novices and guests were all drawn into the pilgrimage to Calvary, for we are all disciples of Jesus and sharing together our human lives and vocations.

From an early period in the Church's history Christians have wished to walk where Jesus walked in the week of his passion. Crowds of pilgrims have achieved this over the centuries, but for the majority it was an unfulfilled dream. The devotion of the 'Stations of the Cross' as a private and corporate practice was developed by Franciscans in the fifteenth century, for Franciscans have always been aware of St Francis' immense desire to enter into the pain and joy of Calvary which led him ultimately to the experience of stigmata.

It is a devotion which contemporary Christians, catholic and evangelical are sharing. It is particularly a Friday devotion, especially during the Fridays of Lent, and most especially on Good Friday. It is a biblical way, though we are not expressly told that Jesus fell under the weight of his cross in scripture, and the story of Veronica wiping Jesus' face is not found in the gospels. The former may be presumed, and the latter may be thought of figuratively in ecumenical gatherings. The devotion calls for a childlike simplicity and heartfelt love for Christ.

It may be adapted in a number of ways, in a church which

displays the stations (or not) or in the open air. The form given here is the one we have traversed this morning, and if you could have walked up the monastery track in the sunshine you would have heard the singing and praying of the friars going from station to station, and looking up you would have seen the words which are engraved below our bell tower: 'There stood at the cross of Jesus Mary, his mother.' It is traditional to sing verses of the *Stabat Mater* hymn (by Franciscan Jacapone da Todi) between each station. This identifies us with Mary the mother of Jesus, focusing on the profound sorrow which she felt in the passion and death of her dear Son who was also her Saviour. And in the sense that she is the image of the Church, we stand with her and St John at the foot of the cross:

> Upon that cross of Jesus
> My eye at times can see
> The very dying form of One
> Who suffered there for me;
> And from my smitten heart, with tears
> Two wonders I confess:
> The wonder of his glorious love,
> And my unworthiness.

Ramon SSF,
Glasshampton Monastery.

The Order for the Stations of the Cross

This devotion may be undertaken alone, with a small group of friends or in a more formal manner within the context of congregational worship. It has a basic simplicity, so that one person, with this book, can complete the stations alone. He can make the pilgrimage 'in the heart' while remaining in one place. But it is better to mark the stations outwardly, either by following them around a church, or in the open air by marking fifteen points with stones or wooden markers.

If it is done in a group, one person should act as Officiant and another (or others) act as Reader/s. If it is part of the normal liturgical worship the particular local practice will be observed. For the sake of this book, I shall presume that it is a group exercise, with an Officiant and a Reader, with the group making the responses and singing the hymns. Traditionally there have been fourteen stations, but it is now a widespread practice to include the fifteenth station in anticipation of the Resurrection.

The pattern for the stations follows. After the *Preparation* each station follows the same order, the *Conclusion* following the fifteenth station. The whole exercise takes from forty-five minutes to an hour, depending upon the length of the reflective silences.

May you enter into the love and compassion of Christ as with body, mind and spirit you follow the Way of the Cross.

11

Jesus is Condemned to Death

1. GROUP gathers at the First Station

2. OFFICIANT reads Scripture: Isaiah 53:3–6

He was despised and rejected by men; a man of sorrows and acquainted with grief; and as one from whom men hide their faces he was despised, and we esteemed him not.

Surely he has borne our griefs and carried out sorrows; yet we esteemed him stricken, smitten by God, and afflicted.

But he was wounded for our transgressions, he was bruised for our iniquities; upon him was the chastisement that made us whole, and with his stripes we are healed.

All we like sheep have gone astray; and have turned every one to his own way; and the LORD has laid on him the iniquity of us all.

3. OFFICIANT: Let us pray:

In the name of the Father, and of the Son, and of the Holy Spirit. Amen.

Our Heavenly Father: On this day we follow our Lord Jesus on the Way of the Cross. Help us in body, mind and spirit to accompany him through his passion and death to his resurrection glory. And help us to remember that as we follow our path through the wilderness of this world we are sustained and comforted by your love, and empowered to show your compassion to others. Through Jesus Christ our Lord . . . Amen.

4. HYMN: **When I Survey**
　　　　　(Tune: Rockingham)

When I survey the wondrous Cross
　　On which the Prince of Glory died,
My richest gain I count but loss,
　　And pour contempt on all my pride.

Forbid it, Lord, that I should boast
　　Save in the death of Christ my God;
All the vain things that charm me most
　　I sacrifice them to his blood.

See from his head, his hands, his feet,
　　Sorrow and love flow mingled down;
Did e'er such love and sorrow meet,
　　Or thorns compose so rich a crown?

Were the whole realm of nature mine,
　　That were a present far too small;
Love so amazing, so divine
　　Demands my soul, my life, my all.

5. FIRST STATION: Jesus is Condemned to Death

OFFICIANT: We adore you, O Christ, and we bless you

PEOPLE: **Because by your holy cross you have redeemed the world.**

READER: You are the Light of the World, Lord Jesus; but men preferred darkness to light. Where there was sickness, gloom, depression and suffering, you brought healing, light, cheer and hope. Your heart overflowed with love and compassion for a lost and needy world, and you did not hold yourself back, but gave yourself completely in love. And then,

14

at last, despised and rejected, you were condemned to death. The very voices that cried 'Hosanna' were poisoned by political and religious authorities to cry 'Crucify'.

Not all the water in the world could wash clean the hands of Pilate or the heart of Caiaphas.

But your compassion and forgiveness included even them. And even me!

6. PAUSE for reflection

7. STANZA of the *Stabat Mater* while group follows Officiant to the next Station:

> At the Cross her station keeping,
> Stood the mournful Mother weeping,
> Close to Jesus at the last.

Stabat Mater (887.D)

Jesus Takes up His Cross

OFFICIANT: We adore you, O Christ, and we bless you

PEOPLE: **Because by your holy Cross you have redeemed the world**

READER: You knew, Lord Jesus, that the shadow of the Cross lay always across your path and over your life. You knew when the Father's word sounded from heaven and when the Holy Spirit came upon you in your baptism, that this path of loving service carried you toward the Cross. But the Cross of pain and suffering which you embraced was the means of salvation and forgiveness for us.

   May we receive our cross and follow you, finding not only the sorrow of Calvary, but the joy and compassion of service.

> Through her soul, of joy bereavèd,
> Bowed with anguish, deeply grievèd,
>   Now at length the sword has passed.

Jesus Falls the First Time

OFFICIANT: We adore you, O Christ, and we bless you

PEOPLE: **Because by your holy Cross you have redeemed the world**

READER: You stumbled, you staggered, you fell—exhausted in the dust. You, by whose word the heavens were made,—you, whose word of command could still the storms, could heal the leper, could raise the dead—you fell exhausted in the dust.

And so I stumble—and stagger—and fall. Help me to know that you have been there before me. Help me to look to you for strength and forgiveness, to get up, and go on again.

> O, that blessèd one, grief-laden,
> Blessèd Mother, blessèd Maiden,
> Mother of the all-holy One.

Jesus Meets His Mother

OFFICIANT: We adore you, O Christ, and we bless you

PEOPLE: **Because by your holy Cross you have redeemed the world**

READER: What wonder is this? Your mother, Lord, who held you in her womb, who pressed you to her breast, who cradled you in her arms,—she beholds you treading the *Via Dolorosa*, the Way of Sorrows. Your mother, who heard the prophecy of Simeon that a sword should pierce her own soul, begins the pain of its fulfilment,—so helpless, and yet still holding you in her heart.

Let me enter into the depths of your sorrows as she did; enable me to feel the sorrows of the world, and to allow your redeeming love to fill me as she did. And with her let me bear you in my heart.

> O that silent, ceaseless mourning,
> O those dim eyes never turning
> From that wondrous, suffering Son.

Simon of Cyrene Helps to Carry Jesus' Cross

OFFICIANT: We adore you, O Christ, and we bless you

PEOPLE: **Because by your holy Cross you have redeemed the world**

READER: It is a very wonderful thing, Lord, that you have need of us, as you had need of the help of Simon of Cyrene. It is clear that we have need of you, for we are creatures and you are the Lord; we are sinful and you are loving and holy. Yet you have need of us, of our love, of our care, of our service.

Sometimes I wonder how I can truly love and serve you, and then I see that it is in giving my heart and my hands to my neighbour and to my enemy that I can serve and love you. You have told us to bear one another's burdens and so fulfil the law of Christ, and you have told us to love and pray for our enemies.

As Simon carried your Cross for you, so help us to ease your load by giving and receiving help ourselves.

> Who on Christ's dear Mother gazing,
> In her trouble so amazing,
>   Born of woman, would not weep?

Veronica Wipes the Face of Jesus

OFFICIANT: We adore you, O Christ, and we bless you

PEOPLE: **Because by your holy Cross you have redeemed the world**

READER: I think about Veronica and wonder if I could have done what she did. How long did she watch you, struggle along in the crowd to be near you, long to reach out a loving hand to help you? At last came the opportunity and she took the linen cloth and wiped from your brow and face the dust and sweat and blood.

The story says that your image was imprinted on the cloth. Perhaps it was. Certainly it must have been impressed on Veronica's heart and mind. When I look upon you, gaze upon you, on the Way of Sorrows and upon your Cross, I feel the image of your humanity and suffering impressed upon my heart. I pray that the image of your glory may also be imprinted there.

> Who on Christ's dear Mother thinking,
> Such a cup of sorrow drinking,
> Would not share her sorrow deep?

Jesus Falls the Second Time

OFFICIANT: We adore you, O Christ, and we bless you

PEOPLE: **Because by your holy Cross you have redeemed the world**

READER: You were determined to go this way. You were not cornered and compelled and caught in the net of the civil and religious authorities. No, you always knew the direction, the shadow of the Cross, the hill of Golgotha, the place of a skull.

And now it has come to this,—falling and staggering a second time, almost unable to go on,—but there's no turning back now, no faltering of spirit, no change of mind or heart. Whatever the cost of our salvation you were prepared, for having loved your own, you loved them to the end.

This is not the stuff that I am made of,—and yet there are times when your love fills my heart, when your courage is made available to me. Oh, may I not fall and fail in the hour that you call me.

> For his people's sins, in anguish,
> There she saw the victim languish,
>   Bleed in torments, bleed and die.

Jesus Consoles the Women of Jerusalem

OFFICIANT: We adore you, O Christ, and we bless you

PEOPLE: **Because by your holy Cross you have redeemed the world**

READER: They wept in their own powerlessness Lord, because feeling for you, they could do nothing but weep. And you! You had an ear and a heart for their pain. You told them to weep for their own sins—as you tell me.

I understand in small part that it was my sins which led you to the Cross, that I had my part in nailing you there. I am quick to think about others' sins, and to judge them—but oh, so slow to allow my own heart to be broken. If I really understood, I would weep for my own sins, for the hurt and pain I have caused you. Perhaps that would relieve your own pain.

> Saw the Lord's anointed taken;
> Saw her Child in death forsaken;
> Heard his last expiring cry.

Jesus Falls the Third Time

OFFICIANT: We adore you, O Christ, and we bless you

PEOPLE: **Because by your holy Cross you have redeemed the world**

READER: This journey which seemed endless is at last reaching its goal. Will you make it? I cannot envisage your death by exhaustion before you reach Calvary,—no, there is something imperative and foreordained about the Cross. But you have fallen for the third time, and you have little strength left.

Perhaps I shall know times when I will wonder if I have enough strength to go on. Certainly I meet people who have come to the end of themselves. But as you were enabled to take those last few steps, so you will give me the strength and resolution needed. Help me to travel one day at a time, one hour at a time—to live in the present moment of your love and grace, for you will never leave me nor forsake me.

> In the passion of my Maker,
> Be my sinful soul partaker,
>   May I bear with her my part.

Jesus is Stripped of His Garments

OFFICIANT: We adore you, O Christ, and we bless you

PEOPLE: **Because by your holy Cross you have redeemed the world**

READER: There was not much else they could take from you, Lord. You had nowhere to lay your head. You expended your love and your strength in the service of others, and now they take away your clothes. You are to be stripped of all, and in dying, be buried as a naked grain of wheat.

How cluttered is my life, and how fearful I am of being stripped of self and sin and pride. I see that having put one's step on the Calvary road, it leads to this, with nothing between you and your Cross. Lord, have mercy on me!

> Of his passion bear the token,
> In a spirit bowed and broken
>   Bear his death within my heart.

Jesus is Nailed to the Cross

OFFICIANT: We adore you, O Christ, and we bless you

PEOPLE: **Because by your holy Cross you have redeemed the world**

READER: I don't understand the depths to which humanity can sink. They take you, Jesus, and slowly, consciously, deliberately, nail you to the cross—hands and feet, in the course of duty. They were merely obeying orders. But whose orders? What malign power lay with the authorities, and what dark, cosmic plotting lay behind such earthly power? And you submit, and not only so, but you pray for those who nailed *(hurt)* you,—for those who ordered them to do so.

   Your last hours manifested only love; love in darkness, love in weakness, love in suffering,—always, only love. If this is so, then the victory must remain with love!

> May his wounds both wound and heal me,
> He enkindle, cleanse, anneal me,
>   Be his Cross my hope and stay.

Nothing could stop you loving.
'The darkness has not overcome it!'
                              (John. 1 .5')
'Love never fails.' (1 Cor. 13 8-)
'By His wounds we are healed.' see (Isaiah 53.5.)

35

TWELFTH STATION:

Jesus Dies upon the Cross

OFFICIANT: We adore you, O Christ, and we bless you

PEOPLE: **Because by your holy Cross you have redeemed the world**

READER: How strange is your passivity, Lord. You have yielded yourself up to the will of men, and given yourself to the will of God. And yet you are accomplishing something. And that 'something' is the salvation of the world. I cannot understand it, measure its height or fathom its depth,—but it is a great and mighty task, an incomprehensible work of love.

Three dark, long hours of suffering, ending in a cry which signified a finished work, and a life commended to the Father. I tremble when I look upon your death, and tremble when I think about my own. Be with me now, Lord Jesus, and in the hour of my death.

> May he, when the mountains quiver,
> From that flame which burns for ever
> Shield me on the judgement day.

Jesus is Taken from the Cross and Given to His Mother

OFFICIANT: We adore you, O Christ, and we bless you

PEOPLE: **Because by your holy Cross you have redeemed the world**

READER: It is over now. All the pain, the suffering, the heartache and the shedding of your precious blood. It is all over now. Your body is taken down tenderly from the Cross, and the nails are removed from hands and feet. Your poor body, scourged, beaten, exhausted and crucified, is now at rest. And at last, your Mother, dear Mary, takes you in her arms, as she did so long ago. You were helpless then, and she knew a sword would pierce her own soul. And now it has come to pass, and you are helpless again.

In the days of your infancy, helplessness gave way to growth, strength and maturity, and to a life lived out in the fullness of its strength for others. And now? Well just now, Mary holds you in her arms in thankfulness, in motherly love, and even in hope . . .

> Jesu, may thy Cross defend me,
> And thy saving death befriend me,
> Cherished by thy deathless grace.

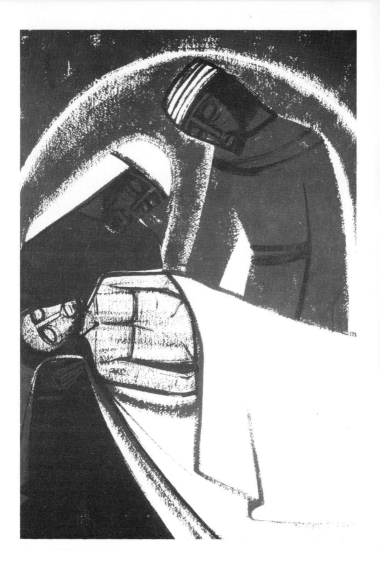

The Body of Jesus is Laid in the Tomb

OFFICIANT: We adore you, O Christ, and we bless you

PEOPLE: Because by your holy Cross you have redeemed the world

READER: Jesus, you are really dead. Your body is cold and lifeless—and your spirit? There is a witness which says that while your body rested in the tomb your spirit traversed the dark places of Hades, bringing light and hope into the darkness. Light appeared in the dark places of the underworld as you harrowed hell and searched for our first parents to lead them up on high, leading captivity captive and giving gifts to men.

So there is silence in the fragrant tomb where your body lies still and alone in strange anticipation. But in the world of spirit there is enkindled a light which shall never be quenched, and the Lord, the Spirit of Life, moves in cosmic darkness, breathing life and light and love.

> When to dust my dust returneth,
> Grant a soul that to thee yearneth
>   In thy Paradise a place.

Jesus Rises from the Dead

OFFICIANT: We adore you, O Christ, and we bless you

PEOPLE: **Because by your holy Cross you have redeemed the world**

READER: The stone had been rolled across the entrance to the tomb. Pilate's seal was set, and the soldiers kept their watch. It seemed to the disciples and to the world at large that you had become a prisoner in the kingdom of the dead. It had finally come to an end.

But life began to stir within the tomb before the rising of the sun. The pure light of the Holy Spirit began to shine, and your body, Lord Jesus, loosed from its imprisoning bands of myrrh and ointments, came forth in risen glory. The boundless energy of your new and immortal life burst the bands of death, rolled the stone away, blinded the soldiers and greeted the lesser sun of creation in its rising.

We remember, today, all the sorrows of Calvary, and feel the grief in our own hearts. But we look for the empty tomb, the glorious rising, eternal life as a present gift and grace, and the life of the world to come.

'I AM He who lives and was dead, says the Lord, and behold, I am alive for evermore, and have the keys of hell and of death. . . .'

8. HYMN: **Jesus Has Died**
      (Tune: Gonfalon Royal)

Jesus has died, the Cross stands bare,
No more can pain and fear molest,
The carpenter His work has done
This sabbath day, and entered rest.

How can the earth breathe in the sun
Heavy with promise of new Spring,
While Christ our God lies cold and still
And His poor Church refuse to sing?

Dark Calvary is shrouded now,
That lonely hill is desolate;
But in the east the far-off light
Glimmers through clouds disconsolate.

The seed is sown in rocky tomb,
The Sun of Righteousness will shine,
The rain of hope waters the earth
And stirs anew the life divine.

Christ's body waits in middle earth,
The Spirit sighs and groans within,
The first day's light of morn will dawn
And break the power of death and sin.

RISE, JESUS, RISE! WE LONG FOR YOU
TO COME AND SET YOUR PEOPLE FREE;
COME NOW, TRIUMPHANT FROM THE GRAVE,
WITH SHOUT AND PALM OF VICTORY!

SSF (R)

9. OFFICIANT reads Scripture: 1 Peter 2:21–25

To this you have been called, because Christ also suffered for
you, leaving you an example, that you should follow in his

steps. He committed no sin; no guile was found on his lips. When he was reviled, he did not revile in return; when he suffered, he did not threaten; but he trusted to him who judges justly. He himself bore our sins in his body on the tree, that we might die to sin and live to righteousness. By his wounds you have been healed. For you were straying like sheep, but have now returned to the Shepherd and Guardian of your souls.

10. OFFICIANT: Let us pray:

Almighty God: we pray you graciously to look upon this your family, for which our Lord Jesus Christ was contented to be betrayed and given up into the hands of wicked men, and to suffer death upon the Cross.

Grant that by his wounds we may be healed, that we may enter into the deep fellowship of his sufferings and death, and rejoice in the power of his resurrection.

In the name of the Father ✝ and of the Son, and of the Holy Spirit. Amen.

11. OFFICIANT: Let us depart in peace.

12. PEOPLE: **In the name of Christ. Amen.**

All depart.

For Holy Saturday

Christ Harrows Hell
(Tune: Gonfalon Royal or LM)

Now while the body, quiet and still
Lies wrapped in bands of linen fair,
The glow of life and warmth and power
Flickers in hell's cold, darkling air.

And while the myrrh and aloes' balm
Perfume his feet and hands and head,
Christ's spreading light pierces the gloom
And lights the kingdom of the dead.

The doors of bronze burst at his cry,
And all the sons of Adam wake,
He harrows hell and breaks death's bonds,
And all the powers of darkness shake.

Adam and Eve, that primal pair
Are led on high to liberty,
While patriarch and prophet stand
And sing the song of jubilee.

The dying thief beholds his Lord,
Fulfilled the promise of the King,
While saints of that first covenant
Join with angelic choirs and sing.

The breaking of the Easter dawn
Reveals the body of the Lord
Endued with life and love and power,
Incarnate is the Eternal Word!

ALL GLORY, CHRIST, OUR RISEN KING,
WHO WITH THE FATHER REIGNS ABOVE
WITHIN THE HOLY SPIRIT'S BOND,
ETERNAL LIFE AND LIGHT AND LOVE.

Amen

SSF (R)

Why This Sudden End?

There is a certain sudden and stark ending to the devotions of the Stations of the Cross. It used to end with Jesus in the tomb . . . darkness . . . waiting . . . hoping. Now, with the fifteenth Station there is a profound sense of anticipation—yet still the shadows of the tomb are around us. Of course, we know that Jesus has risen victoriously from the grave, for he dwells within the believer's heart and in the bosom of the Church. But it is well for us to feel the sorrows of Good Friday in a liturgical sense. We must live through darkness and pain in our earthly lives, and all our hope is mingled with sadness and our joys are mixed with tears. When we celebrate the eucharist we 'show forth' again the Lord's death until he comes (1 Cor. 11:26), and on Good Friday and Holy Saturday we live in the time between our Lord being laid in the cold stillness of the tomb, and the stirring to resurrection life by the Holy Spirit.

Isaac Watts' hymn *When I Survey the Wondrous Cross* portrays the suffering, dying Jesus most movingly before our very eyes, and if we come to the end of the Stations of the Cross with great sorrow in our hearts, that's how it should be. It may be a most appropriate experience to remain there in the sorrows of Jesus, and remember that wherever in our poor world there is sorrow, pain, starvation, famine or suffering of any kind,—there Jesus grieves and weeps and labours again for the salvation of the world, which is 'not yet', but which will be consummated when he comes again in glory.

If you feel the sorrow of Calvary as you complete this devotion, then give thanks for it, affirm faith in the anticipation of the risen Jesus, and hold the sorrows of the world before God in love and prayer. Walking with Jesus on this way of sorrows will enrich and nourish your own pilgrimage of faith, and the light of his Easter rising will radiate from your life, and lighten some dark corner of our world.